JUST ANOTHER MESSENGER OF GOD

MY COUNTY JAIL EXPERIENCES

SIR FINIS DeMILO BREWER

Just Another Messenger of GOD

Copyright 2015

By: SIR FINIS DeMILO BREWER

Published by : TOOSWEETPUBLISHING
+ + +   productions

 P.O.Box 6512 New Orleans, La. 70174 email:
toosweetpublishing@yahoo.com

 website: TOOSWEETPUBLISHING.com

ISBN: 978-0-941091-14-5

First Printing

PRINTED IN THE UNITED STATES OF AMERICA

TABLE OF CONTENTS

My Early Days of Trusting Others...

(When the Bible says: Trust No Man)

The hardest part for me as a Writer when I'm having to remember all the experiences & events in my life that were not the best of times, is reliving each moment as if it was happening all over again. Unfortunately as I write these stories and events in my life, some incidents won't be included because living the experience once was enough; reliving it twice is too much to ask of myself. Plus, sometimes the truth is too hard to bear. And some of things spoken to me, about me, and done to me (by others) over the years, I rather keep between me, them, and GOD. And let Him be the judge. For sometimes people do things and say things that even their mothers & fathers would never believe, and be too ashamed to know. And not wanting to place anyone in a negative "light" intentionally, I'll let "Time" tell their story, instead of me letting the "cat of truth" out of the bag.

For the Bible says, "The Truth will always come out..."So whether you LIE, or whether you HIDE, it's just a matter of time that who you really are, will all be revealed in the END...

...And as one of GOD's many Messengers, time will also tell

if a Heavenly place, or Hellish One

is where you will find your Soul

when YOU leave this PLACE.

I TIMOTHY 5:14-15

"I will therefore that the younger women marry, bear children, guide the house, give none occasion to the adversary to speak reproachfully. For some are already turned aside after satan."

In my very short time as a Minister called of GOD, I've had some very profound and very interesting experiences. Praying without ceasing, fasting, and casting out demons, had become the norm for me. Spending time in jail had become another addition to my list of experiences as a Messenger of the Gospel of CHRIST here in 2012.

Jesus spent a bit of time in jail; John the Baptist was beheaded while incarcerated; and the Apostle Paul found freedom from his confinement on one occasion with the help of an Angel of GOD.

My own jail experiences however, were all tied to failed marriages. Demonically influenced marriages that were great at first, then turned to "Hell on earth." All with divine warnings sent by GOD beforehand. But unfortunately, neither of them listened, or wanted anything more to do with GOD. Two wives almost 7 years apart; and two failed marriages twelve years apart. But the same Devil, same evil spirit (Lust), using the same method that he always use to destroy covenant relationships (Deception). Yet many do not know that nothing has changed since the Garden of Eden. Satan is still lying to the "daughters of Eve" and they are still listening to him. Falling for the same old LIES, SAME OLD TRICKS, same M.O. Deceiving them into thinking, and believing he has a better plan for their life, and can make them happier.

Well, coming from someone who knows;... No devil can offer you anything worthwhile. And no one knows what's best for you other than the GOD that created you. Your own mother & father don't even know what's best for you. That's why as parents, its best we pray and ask GOD for help & guidance...when it comes to the destiny of our children. And especially, when it comes to our marriages.

STUMBLING INTO

MY FIRST MARRIAGE

My first wife was a choice I made, and looking back I can see now the many clear signs indicating that I should not have taken that "road". But at the time, I had known her most of her life, she was in trouble, and I knew the history of her and her mother's constant strife.

When she was about 10 or 11 years old, her and my younger brother was "going together". I don't know how much you can do at 10 or 11 years of age, but no one takes a relationship serious at that age; at least at the time I didn't. Of course her and I getting together later caused quite a buzz in both families, but it was not planned. Matter of fact I was best friends with her first cousin, and in love with her other first cousin, and had been for the past 5 years. I know it all sounds like a "soap opera" but that was my life back then…

…Somebody was always liking (me) "Finis" and "Finis" was always secretly liking somebody else. It just didn't seem fair, but that's how life was for me growing up. I had lots of female friends, but only one "girlfriend" at a time. I knew I wanted to be married one day, so if I didn't start a problem while I was young, it wouldn't be a problem when I got older.

Nothing ever became of the love I had for my wife's cousin, and probably explained a lot of my behavior following our "emotional breakup." Even though she was only a year younger than my wife, her home life was a lot more stable. And a lot less likely of creating a situation that might untimely force us together. She went on to have a normal life, graduating from school, marrying someone in the military and starting a family of her own; never really knowing just how much she meant to me, or affected my life. But that was so long ago.

But so was Niecy, and the two other Karens, Georgina, Ida, Sybil, Jenni in Bunkie, LA. Jerline in the "Cut-off" and at least 10 other PYT's that never knew they inspired me.

As for my wife, her life was a classic case of child abuse, and no one seemed to care. Even now, almost twenty years later, she and her mother still don't see eye to eye. Being under the same roof for more than a day usually is a fuss waiting to happen. She is the grandmother of my first set of children, and at one point she offer to pay someone to kill me; because she hated me so. But it didn't bother me. I know if you trust & live your life as GOD see fit,

"NO weapon formed against you shall prosper".

I learned about this plot years later from her daughter; we were still married at the time. Her mother even lived with us for a few weeks. But that's "mad Max" for ya; I ain't mad with her. I'd still do anything for her, because she is my children's grandmother.

After I divorced her daughter, she realized just how good of a husband I was to her only daughter.

When the 1st wife and I first got together, I had found out her mother had put her out on the street yet again. She was by some strangers she hardly knew. Having known her since she was a kid, I couldn't just ignore the danger she may have put herself in. So I called the mother to get her side of the story, and with very little concern, she went on to say,

"Yea I put that "so and so out… She just lie all the time…blah blah blah…and no she can't come back here."

Hanging up, I was stunned; but not surprised. This was normal for Max…to put her under age daughter out on the street. Having known and been associated with this family for a few years, this behavior was nothing new.

My wife was known to lie a lot as a child, but the apple didn't fall far from the tree. No one could fabricate a story like her mom "Mad max".

Looking back, I've learn to over-look some things about people; even Max. I'm sure she was also the product of not the greatest life growing up; even heard she was married by 13.

When I made the decision to go back to California and hopefully catch up with my eldest brother, I said to my wife whom I was only friends with at that time,

"Hey look, I'm going to California. You are welcome to come if you like. You really shouldn't be where you are; you hardly know the people"

And having already been turned away by her Aunts & older cousins, a few weeks later her & I left for the West Coast. Being 23 years old, had my own car (a cool, all white '79 T-Bird that was very well known in the neighborhood), we prepared to leave New Orleans behind. I had agreed to drive my cousin's sister-in-law back to Arizona. I had never met her, and didn't know anything about her. But I wasn't working anywhere at the time so I said,

"What the heck;...It's just   another adventure."

My cousin's husband was supposed to drive his sister and her kids back home, but he backed out. So me being bored, & the economy in 1985 was the dumps, I agreed to drop her off in Flagstaff, Arizona. And then we would head on to the West Coast.

Having only just met the benefactor of my kindness, I didn't have a problem driving her and her 4 kids back to Arizona. Going out of the way for complete strangers was normal for me. Plus, she had just buried her children's father, and didn't have enough money to catch the plan back home. So I volunteered to bring her. She buy the gas, I provide the car. The long car ride was the only economical option to us both getting to where we were going. And after dropping our new friend & her kids off in Flagstaff, Arizona, the wife and I went on to California.

Unfortunately I wasn't able to catch up with my brother, so I stayed by my niece's family for a few days. Then I called our "new friend" (Shelia) in Flagstaff, and asked if we could come back by her. It was pointless to return to New Orleans.

"Hey Shelia, you mind if we come back and stay by you a while? I couldn't find my brother, and don't know how to reach him..."

Sheila gladly agreed, and for the next ten years, my wife & I spent a life married, living in a town we had never seen or heard of before. Black people were rare, and small town living was something new for both of us. My brother told me years later that the FBI called looking for me; I just laughed. "Mad Max' would help her daughter, but she would go out of her way to make her life miserable. I didn't worry about the call; I had to trust GOD to protect me & her both, because I couldn't just leave her in the street with complete strangers. Ain't no telling what would have happen to her. Oftentimes, people don't want to get involve, but I'm not one of those kind of people.

Flagstaff, Arizona was a small college town, overshadowed by the well-known university (NAU). A small town where it seem like to me,…nothing ever happened. And nothing was going to happen. Things were so slow and behind the times compared to New Orleans, that I used to say,

"Man, when the world comes to an end, Flagstaff will find out a year later".

And to see another black person…It was like spotting a UFO; that's how rare we saw them.

We had a great life in Flagstaff, and I met lots of great friends, like Sandy & Marietta; Kathy & her dad Mr Ruiz; Ann & Rudy and the kids; and of course Woody from Denny's. All my neighbors out on Leupp Rd like: Ralph &

Ginger, Louie & Lori and the kids, other family like Mama Yazzie, and all my Navajo sisters, Debra, Dina, Annette, Tina, & Toni, and brother Jimmie & Marvin. It was such a good life out on those 14.9 acres…paid for free & clear.

But all good things eventually come to a close though; the quiet and simply life ended. And we returned back to New Orleans at the voice and instruction of Almighty GOD. This was home for us; even though all our children were born in Arizona and are considered Arizona natives. They loved it there; and if I had anything to say in the matter, they all would have all spent Summers in New Orleans, and would have continue growing up and finish school in Flagstaff.

When the Lord called me to the Ministry, the voice was loud and clear, and definitely that of GOD.

"…I want you to go back home to New Orleans," HE said.

These were the very first words that the LORD spoke to me. And called me not only to the Ministry; but also HOME to New Orleans. And this is where my Life,

…began to get crazy.

It's been a rough ride over the years, but I didn't know GOD like I know HIM now. So I made a few mistakes during my younger days. But being called to the Ministry for me was never a mistake. It may have been for my wife because it didn't take long for her to commit adultery, and forever change the family that we had made together.

Soon after arriving back in that city we both grew up in, and that is often referred to as "The Big Easy" by most tourist, life as we knew it became far from easy.

In spite of GOD not making the choice, this marriage produced 3 sons and two daughters that I'm very proud of and love dearly. We never wanted for much because of GOD's covenant to married people, and I believe because of his promises to "Servants." We enjoyed all the benefits that came with this very special class of "sexually active" people. But because we sometimes marry people we shouldn't (not GOD's choice), marriages will more than likely end. Even after being together 15 years, ours ended, and was very unpleasant. I believe as adults, we could have sat down an amicable sever our covenant since she obviously had it in her heart to end the marriage. But instead she ran off with the neighbor who lived across the street from us. And he was "slime bucket" when it came to screwing and using women. But that's what she wanted..."Captain whoremonger over Prince Charming." Now I'm not bragging, but I know I was/is a good-man, good husband, and a GODly loving father to my children. And all the Lying crooked Judges, Lawyers, ex-family members, jailers, detectives, & blind CPS workers can "kiss my Ass" for painting a different picture of me otherwise. Just as I witness it all; so did GOD; and HE WILL be the judge, jury, & decide their fate in the end. For HE said,

"Vengeance is mine; I will repay"

(To the professions mentioned above; If you believe in your heart of hearts you were fair & just in dealing with Sir Finis D. Brewer, then the "kiss my Ass" doesn't apply to you)

After being lied on, robbed of all the work and sacrifices to raise a good family, and my name & reputation slandered, there was nothing left of a great example of "family." Even after petitioning for custody of my children, and the fact that the Law clearly states that "in the best interest of the children" determines the custody, the "father/man-hating" justice system still gave the children to the cheating wife, with the new boyfriend that was a womanizer, pill popper, drinker, and Hoe.

Just Another Messenger of GOD

I tried to warn the wife that she was making a mistake, but she wouldn't listen. Even after GOD gave several warnings, and even gave instructions before hand to avoid the destructions of the marriage, the wife insisted on doing what she wanted. And not what GOD would rather. But this is very typical of a soul deceived by a Lust spirit.

At the time, I was a youth Pastor in the church where we were, and she was head of the Praise team in our little church of less than a hundred members. I found out later that the manner in which she became possessed by this Lust spirit was due to her presence at a strip club while I was out of town. One of many places I call "Satan's territories".

Some believe there is no harm in going to, or being in certain places where people in the world love to dwell. But over the years I've learned that there are certain places as Christian we should not patronize, and definitely not possess a desire or curiosity to experience. While I was out of town trying to get things ready for our move back to Arizona, I learn that during my wife's few nights of partying while I was away, she join a family member for a girl's night out at this strip club. And when you are where Satan dwells, and his works can be found, you'll subject yourself to the devil's very destructive influences. For as the Bible says,

"...for Satan has come to steal, kill, and to destroy."

There is a lot more I could say here, but you can read about it in one of many other books I'm working on. It's old news now, but the hurt and damage was undeniable. After going before a judge who I later learn was more unrighteous than just, I was surprisingly ordered to give the wife a car because I had several. I felt that since she was so bent on leaving, and running around with another man, that it was no longer her car. As far as I was concern, her "man" could provide her with transportation. My generosity toward her was now dried up. And whether she walked, or crawl, it didn't matter to me. She should have made sure the guy she chose to "throw her life away with" had more than one vehicle…when she decided to be a whore, and no longer a wife. But these dumb, foolish women don't think before they make these stupid, and life destroying decision. If they were thinking at all, they would have made a better choice, and the world would be a better place. And if the judge that I stood before was a true instrument of justice, he too would have made a more righteous decision concerning the wife & I. Instead, he was the first to open my eyes to this unjust & bias profession. This rather obvious corrupt, and farce system of justice that don't seem to be bothered by immorality, lying under oath, or lying Lawyers. A system where with a little practice, the Truth should be as easily to distinguish from a Lie, as light is from darkness. But this judge in a gender bias & racially motivated decision sentenced me unjustly to my very first experience behind bars.

ORLEANS PARISH JAIL

Sentenced to 6 months in jail, and $10,000 fine for contempt of court, I was immediately seized by the bailiff, hand-cuffed, and taken to the back to start my shocking sentence. Fuming with anger and disbelief, my last words to the judge was,

"You're not GOD..."

As the wife looked on standing next to some guy I never seen before, she obviously was feeling vindicated.

I later learn the guy that was with her was the brother of the man she was now sleeping with, and leaving me for. While slandering my name before this judge, and saying I was abusive. To my shock and surprise, her new boyfriend was the truck driver who lived across the street from us for the past 4 years. Of course, the incident was the talk of the neighbors for a very long time. Especially when she moved in this house with this slime-bucket. And, with my kids. A House directly sitting across the street from our own house… at 908 Sumner St. Where her and I had lived with our children for 5 years prior. I'm sure many was thinking, and saying,

"…What the hell was going through her head! Ain't no Sex that damn good to be made that big of a damn fool!"

After being arrested and placed in the holding cell, I sat in the jail on the floor with my blood boiling. I could not believe that a system I once respected and held in such high regard, was now a figure of unrighteousness & hypocrisy in my mind. I would never be able to look at this "so-called system of justice" the same. But then why was I surprised, even the Bible warns us as Christians about our court system. It tells us to avoid it at all cost, because it loves money and not justice. And it won't let you go until it bleeds you dry…of course I'm paraphrasing, but the message is unmistakable.

After being locked up in jail, all my new cellmates wasn't shy about telling me that,

"If a Judge gives you 6 months, you gonna do 6 months."

I said,

"Not happening!...The GOD I serve is not gonna allow me to serve no 6 months when I ain't done nothing wrong...My GOD ain't gonna allow it!"

Settling down in jail, I met a few new friends; share the Gospel of Jesus Christ with all that wanted to hear it, and was even proposition by a cellmate. He offered to take care of my little problem; he even bragged about having a "graveyard" out there beyond those iron bars. In other words, these were the recipients of his ability to commit murdered. He would consider it an honor, to do this little favor for me.

As mad as I was, I admit I found the proposition a bit tempting, but being the true "Man of GOD" that I am, I know it was just satan being satan. And using his many "lost ones" that blindly give themselves over to his deeds. I soon reminded him (and myself) that GOD says,

"Vengeance is mine, I will repay!"

And since I already knew that GOD is a God of his Word, and HE will do exactly what HE say, I had no problem letting HIM handle my situation. I didn't call it a problem, because problems to me don't have solutions. And knowing GOD like I do, there is no such thing as a problem in GOD's realm. When we pray…

"…problem solved!"

While I survived my very first time in jail, and thanks to GOD, I never stayed 6 months or paid a $10,000 dollar fine. I was incredibly release in only 41 days.

After being incarcerated for 2 or 3 weeks, I was wrecking my brain trying to figure out how I was to get out of this hell hole. I was tempted to write a letter to this judge and apologize, but GOD said,

"NO!"

From this, GOD taught that when you are right, you never have kiss the butt of an unrighteous person. Or, take back what was said to them, if you said it according to the Word of GOD, and they are wrong in what they are asking you to do. Even if the person you said it to,

…IS A JUDGE.

Right is Right; Wrong is Wrong!

I also learned that when you stand on the Word of GOD, GOD will back up HIS own Word, and deal with the unrighteous person in HIS own time.

So after getting my hands on the Law books, and learning about the Law as it pertained to my particular case, I wrote a petition to this unrighteous judge. Already being familiar with petitions & civil procedures, I was quite comfortable with forwarding this legal longhand written document to the courts. In the past I've had to represent myself in court several times, and have learned certain procedural & court practices. I learned (and I'm ashamed to say) that outside of money, most attorney care nothing about the facts of the case, or JUSTICE. The truth of the matter is, if you know how to LIE, you'll be right at home in most courtrooms.

I've also learned over the years that even in the most well respected firms, LYING seems to be a perquisite.

So due to this rather successful petition I filed from jail, it got me a hearing before this same judge. And thanks to GOD, this hearing got me freed from jail in only 41 days.

I stood before the same judge, and he read from the transcript what was said to him several weeks earlier as I was being carted off to jail. And after reading back to me, the few statements I made about him not being GOD, I was given instructions by the Holy Spirit not to say a single word. I actually thought I was going to have to say something to defend my case, but I stood there silent. Then he said,

"Mr Brewer, you are free to go."

I watched as my once lovely wife nearly passed out as he read the verdict, and released me from jail. She was standing in the back with her brother, and probably had the boyfriend standing outside the courtroom. It really didn't matter to me at that point who she was with, or who she was dating. All I know I was free, and didn't give a damn if she was dating Donald Duck & Mickey Mouse both, or sleeping with Tom, Dick, & Harry. Her Lies, and attempt at slandering my name tried to destroy me...but GOD said,

"Not So!"

(,,,touch not my Anointed, and do my Prophet no harm!)

While in jail, I lost several houses (3) and many cars (20), job opportunities and income. And my lovely children were forever taken from me, and given custody to a foolish female. Who couldn't the difference from the King she left, for the Joker she was now excited about. And a Joker he was.

My kids have suffered greatly in the end because of this Judge's order. Oftentimes people don't think about the price of sin, before they sin. They don't realize that Sin comes with a very high price. This ex-wife has suffered everyday with sickness & aches and pains since she did what she did to me more than 15 years ago. She has had many chances to fix it, and remove the curse but she hasn't. So she suffers even now as I write. Many times the Lord has had me to pray for her. But healing will never come to anyone, when you still have hatred and bitterness in your heart. She the one that left, but she can't stand me because…I survived.

Young people of today; know this when it comes to the SIN that you so love & call FUN…

SIN WILL...take you places you don't want to go & will later regret;

...It will also make you pay a price you cannot afford;

...and lose things you cannot replace;

(like Time, and your children's   precious moments)

...And Sin will sometime leave you gravely ill;

Or, just plain dead.

"Seems to me, the pleasure... just isn't worth the pain."

MEETING MY YOUNG

& GORGEOUS WIFE

Corinthians 13:1-13

"Though I speak with the tongues of men, and of angels, and have not charity, I am become as sounding brass, or a tinkling cymbal........And now abide Faith, Hope, & Charity, these three; but the greatest of these is CHARITY."

Fast forward almost 12 years; I find myself incarcerated again; but this time it was a different place, a different time, a different wife...But all the same lies & deceptions.

It was October, 2012 when the drama started. This wife unlike the first; was chosen by GOD, and we had the best relationship ever. Like a hand to glove, we were a perfect fit. In spite of our 28 yr age difference, we were a great couple.

No one by looking at us would ever know that we came from different eras. And like most moments in life, when things are going well, you can expect a visit from satan. Well if you are a Christian. Because if you already belong to the devil, and you are already living for him, why would he need to bother you?

But if you claim to be a Christian, and you are not where you suppose to be, are doing what you suppose to be doing, you will become a victim of deceptions. And most, when they are being deceived, don't believe that they are. There is nothing you can tell them; to convince them that they are under demonic influence.

Why "lighting" struck me twice, was for a long time a great mystery to me. Then I thought GOD was trying to teach me about forgiveness. But a friend of mine didn't agree. He felt that GOD would never use Sin to teach us a lesson. So after that conversation, I was a bit perplexed and no longer understood why this "rollercoaster ride of sin" was happening in my life yet again.

Just Another Messenger of GOD

My wife and I were both born in New Orleans. She in a area called Harvey; I in an area called Algiers. We came together after the aftermath of Hurricane Katrina. We were from different worlds, and our paths would have never crossed under normal circumstances, but Hurricane Katrina created many extenuating circumstances for thousands of people who once called New Orleans home…And ours situation was no different.

The first time I saw my wife, I was visiting a friend in another part of the city. I had been divorced and was living as a celibate bachelor for the past 5 plus years, with no particular plans for a new wife. But during one of my rough & lonely times, I cried out to the LORD and said,

"GOD, I do not want to be a bachelor forever, so could you please choose a wife for me. And where ever she is right now, I want to meet her before our time."

Well…me with my big mouth, and with these words, I set a "ball into motion". Like so many of the crazy prayers that I've prayed that forever changed my life, this little prayer would also have a great impact on me. Change my life forever; as well as the wife that I was asking GOD to send early. Didn't know where she was; didn't know who she was, but I knew GOD was going to send her. He promise HE would answer my Prayers…

"…the Prayers of a righteous man, availeth much…"

Have you heard of Elijah; the Servant of GOD who prayed that it wouldn't rain, and it didn't. For 6 months; on the whole face of the earth!

You see I studied him early in my childhood years, and he is one of my favorites. Then Samuel; then Jeremiah; and of course, Moses & Abraham.

…When I saw her about a year later (*I have to check my Journals to verify*) I was visiting one of best friends (Gwen) that lived in the area.

Since my first divorce, and not having much contact with my children due to the ex trying to keep them from me, I found myself with a lot of unwanted time on my hand. So I visited my friend often, to keep my mind off the obvious. And I sometimes stopped by my Caucasian family/friends (Angela & RC) whom I had known for about a year or more and who attend the same church I attended. There house was on the corner, and my other friend's house was four houses down.

On this day particular day, as I neared my friend Gwen's house, I notice new neighbors in the house on the corner; right across the street from Angela & RC. I didn't give it much thought, because I didn't pay much attention to the neighborhood. I visited my friend in the area, and didn't pay much attention to anything else. Then one day, other than seeing the mother & father, I saw what I assume was the daughter coming out of the house. Upon seeing her, the first thing I said was,

" GOOD GOD!...who in the world is that!"

I was so taken by the sight, the words were not just a thought in my head, but became an audible sound that escaped my lips. I don't know if my friend heard me, but I'm sure the angels in heaven did. My heart must have awakened that very moment. My divorce had left me literally dead artistically; dormant romantically, and asleep erotically.

Seeing her for the very first time, I hadn't written a poem in years. The divorce had left me with a rather serious case of Writer's block, blind to any possible prospects, and no current "PYT" for literary inspiration. But the moment I saw her, the flood gates were open wide, and the literary pieces that so many have inspired me to write since the age of 12, began to flow again. I began to write like a "hopeless romantic" man who had been sleep for years. And was now awaken by the most gorgeous face...my eyes had ever seen in life.

The title of the very first piece I was inspired to write after seeing my wife from a distance was called

"Those Eyes".

It's an incredible depiction of what I saw & felt when I laid eyes on her for the first time.

"Oh My Lord!"

...were the only words that came to mind.

Other incredible "literary pieces" that were written and inspired by her, can be found in several books I've written. And several pieces I call "Literary Art". You will also find some inspirations in some songs I've written, as well as a few plays, etc. They were all inspired, & dedicated to this lovely time spent while gazing at her from a distance. All the pieces were inspired by her, and I hadn't even come within ten feet of her yet. The only time at this point that I was within 10 feet of her, I was being introduced to her parents as they were sitting on their porch as we walked across the street to say hello. One day after visiting RC & Angela.

My friend Angela thought it would be nice to meet the newest residents to the area; it was so "white" of her. But she couldn't help it; she's my white "sista" living in a black neighborhood…and the only family. So I just tagged along…

"You want to go meet them?"

"Ummm, sure,"

I tried not to show my excitement, as I wondered who this "gorgeous" addition to the neighborhood was, but I was smiling from ear to ear inside.

We made it across the street safely; my friend Angela being the "outgoing friendly white person" living in a black neighborhood had no problem introducing me to her new neighbors across the street from her house.

"This is my friend Sir, and this is Preacher-man, and his wife Betty," was the introduction.

Betty and Angela had a lot in common; they were the only "white women" living within the

area, and I saw that they both were strangely, very comfortable.

As I was being introduced to the parents on one side of the porch, the daughter was on the opposite side of the porch reclining in a chair. With my back turned to her, I turned around to also say hello and found her staring at me sizing me up. She later admitted after we were married, that she was indeed checking me out, and wanted to beat up my friend Angela, because she thought I was sleeping with her.

For the first 8 months I didn't even know her name. And when I learned it later, like my own, it was unique. And when you place the letter of her first name with the first initial of my name, it spelled "U.S." and I thought how cute that was; maybe it was a sign.

Later on it became one of our little inside love symbols we shared. It was also the initials of her first & last name; which I later had placed on the front license plate of my green Mustang convertible I had at the time. It was our little secret code.

After a few weeks of meeting her, her parents were now aware that she was liking me, and they really could not stand my guts even though I hadn't done anything but be myself. Whenever I was visiting my female friends in the neighborhood (Gwen & Angela), and her parents happen to see me, I learned later that many nasty comments were made in reference to me. She even told me much later that her Dad said he was going to throw me in the river, and take my Mustang Convertible…I never understood why he was called Preacher man.

I guess it was assumed that the female friends and I were an item. It was also very obvious that

I was much older guy than their daughter, and they were not happy whenever they saw me across the street. Because by now their daughter could no longer hide her obvious attraction to the "good looking guy" that glanced at her often.

To my great surprise however, I later learned that this lovely object of my affection was still in school, and this disappointed me tremendously because I felt we had no chance of ever meeting, let alone becoming an item. Nevertheless, being a praying man, I began to pray like I always do, and so I prayed,

"Father GOD, I don't know what your plans are, and I don't know if there are any plans for me and this gorgeous person I've seen. But if you would permit, I would love to have her in my life".

"And even though I believe I love her already, if I cannot provide for her, then I rather not have her in my life. I rather not have her, than to have her, and have to struggle."

I also later realized that she reminded me a vision of someone in my dreams as a young boy, with this same beautiful brown skin. And long gorgeous black hair. This vision left me with an obvious attraction to the East Indian race, which exhibit these gorgeous features. It also probably explained my unexplainable attraction to this lovely "PYT" that I now thought of constantly, and found myself inspired to write (non-stop), the most inspirational romantic literary masterpieces ever. Seeing the vision of her in my dream when I was a young boy, I later calculated that it would still be about 17 years before she would even be born, and almost 17 more before she would be eligible to marry. There was a 28 year difference between US, but you would never know it. We got along great, were a perfect couple (and she knew it then, but denies it now), and she also knew GOD brought US together…and it took a Hurricane.

Hurricane Katrina.

So our coming together must have been OUR destiny…for both of U.S.

The one time I got to share one of these lovely inspired creations with her, I thought she would reject me, and find my interest in her offensive. Having learned that she was still in school, I just wanted to let her know that someone thought she was gorgeous, because I believe one should say what they feel... even if the odds are stack against you. For you have more to lose if you say nothing, than to say something and be rejected. So I sent her the poem...

Gorgeous...

It wasn't easy getting a copy of the poem to her, but I managed to do so. To my surprise, she was receptive to it, and had an mutual interest in me as well. This of course was a shock to me, because our paths would never cross under normal circumstances. But remember, me with my big mouth,

...I PRAYED.

...And when I pray, the crazies things happen.

The number of pieces I wrote after looking into "Those beautiful Eyes" of hers must have at least numbered a 100 poems. All new "Romantic pieces". I know this may sound harsh, but in the 15 years I was married and together with my first (children's mother), I wrote only one "piece". I figured I owed myself (and her) that. And I think that can be best explained by the fact that I knew she loved me, but didn't LOVE me. All the years we were together, I felt she wanted to be somewhere else, or with someone else. I can't explain it, but that's what I felt, and I could never shake it. She never liked being affectionate, so I guess , deep down inside, my SOUL knew. And so our marriage eventually ended, and ended horribly.

Now, if I had my say so, my first marriage would have ended like this:

"Ahh Babe, can we talk?"

"Sure."

"You know I love you, and care for you a lot;…but I don't think we should be together anymore."

"Ok..?"

"You can live in one of the Apartments, and I'll live in the big house; the children primarily will live with me, and stay with you on the weekend."

"Ummm?"

"Well it's your idea to split, soooo I keep the children, you keep the car I just bought you, and I keep the new van, and I'll file the papers Monday."

That's how it would have went, and that's how I felt it should have went. No sleazy lawyer, or crooked judge, or sleazy adulterous incidents needed. Judges & lawyers weren't needed when the marriage was consummated, so "3rd parties" are not needed afterwards. And people need to wake up to that fact.

My first marriage was ok, and I would have stayed together forever, because family is important to me. But she wanted out, and so out she went. The 2nd marriage was even better (10x better), until she listened to others and thought someone else could give & love her better. I guess some of US have to learn the hard way that...

"The grass is not (and never will be) greener on the other side; No matter what anyone says."

And to all the females out there that believe it's all about size, I feel sorry for you. Cause if it was that important, GOD would have made sure every man was the same size down there...but he didn't. But even a fool knows that if "a chick just wants you for your dick; she ain't a chick worth having. But even though all pussy feels the same, acts the same, looks the same, there is a difference between a Lady...& a Tramp.

So whether your focus is dicks or dildos, you need a heart transplant, renew your mind, and find JESUS.

The most important thing in life is LOVE; if a man has the "size" but don't give a damn about you, then you're just another "hole"…everybody has one.

Frankly, I'll take love any day. Cause you can be happily married and something happens to your spouse where they cannot be sexual with you anymore…What?

…are you gonna leave them?

If that's who you are (shallow, sorry, vain, ass),…

… what goes around, comes back around, in the end.

I don't know how the first wife feels about her decision now that almost 15 years has passed (about the same time we are together), but if you ask her about that "person" she left me for, she hates him. They are divorce and she shacking with someone else. When I see him, we laugh and talk like nothing ever happen. Why?

…Because that's the kind of person that I AM. GOD's doing; the old me would have accepted the offer in jail.

"Without love or forgiveness, no man can see the kingdom of GOD"

"…I've made my reservation in Heaven; Hell ain't got nuthin for me, and I ain't got nuthin for it. My sins were hung on the "Cross of Calvary". I'm born again, and I'm the "righteousness of GOD."

If you can understand that statement, then no matter what kind of Sin you are in, or have committed, repent, and leave that life, and you can say the same.

The New Wife

Hurricane Katrina came in August 2005, and Life as we knew it was forever changed for both of U.S. She was airlifted out with her mother and brothers to a shelter in Tennessee, and I was still stuck in my office in New Orleans. I specifically knew that I was suppose to stay and ride the hurricane out; and as crazy as it sounds, I did.

I remember my ex calling me on the phone in a panic right before it hit saying,

"Finis, are you staying? I don't know what to do?"

I responded,

"GET MY KIDS OUT OF HERE, THIS ONE IS NOT GONNA BE PRETTY!"

How did I know this?

At that point I remember the three dreams that I'd been having. Even before I heard of a

Hurricane Katrina, I had saw in a dream, downtown Canal Street under water. Three times I had the dream, and at the time I didn't know what it meant. After I learned of the Hurricane, I knew exactly what it meant, and I knew I was suppose to stay and witness it all.

Because I've talked about this in other books, I won't go into great detail here. Fast forward to Texas; this is where my new wife and I are living now. Of course this is a miracle because only 3 months earlier I couldn't even get within 20 feet of her, now we are together. Her mother signed a "Emancipation Affidavit" had it notarized, and we were in the eyes of GOD married (no matter what anyone else said). I put a ring on her finger and our lives were the best.

Being that I've met and have loved so many(only spiritually & emotionally...not sexually) in my life, my life has been pretty good. But if I had only met and known only this wife, and died and never had known another, I would have died a very happy man.

Just Another Messenger of GOD

WHY?...because I know it was GOD's doing; and HE knows best.

She used to get so mad that I had ever been with anyone else, and married before. But I told her,

"It wasn't my fault baby. If I knew you were coming in the world, I wouldn't have left my mama's house till I was 30, and would have waited for you. If I would have just known..."

But I guess I should have known; I had hints. Between 13 and 15 years old, I had a dream. And looking back it was her gorgeous face that I saw. Pretty soft brown skin, long black pretty hair, and the most beautiful eyes I'd ever seen. Crazy isn't it?

But as much as I love my first set of children, I can't imagine my life without them in it...I just can't. And I wouldn't want to imagine such a thing.

Recently, I read several books about the subject of "Past Lives;" the titled is called "Only LOVE is Real." The book just shook me to my very Soul, and it makes some very interesting points as it share some very interesting & true stories. After reading it, and looking back at all that has happened in my life, I know if there is such a thing as "past lives" my wife and I knew each other in "past lives."

I have a brother named Keith; he has been in jail now for a while for stupid things that doesn't warrant the time he has served, or has been sentenced to serve. GOD gave me a revelation one day that brought me to tears, and I had to apologize to GOD (and to my brother even if it was in the spirit). GOD showed me that if I had never been with my 1st wife, my brother probably wouldn't be in jail. And that revelation "broke my heart" cause I just had never made the connect to his "troubles". Maybe they were connect to his love for his "childhood girlfriend". It hurt me to the core of my very soul thinking that my actions may have indirectly put my brother in jail. I love him, and I know he doesn't belong in there.

I love my children though, (it's hard to even imagine not having my children...too hard to imagine) but if I could turn back the clock, I would have never married their mother...if it would have kept my brother out of jail. If I only knew then, what I know now...

From this I've learned just how intimate each life can, and is connected. There actually may be something to this "past lives" stuff; I don't believe they (those who believe) have all the pieces, but there is something to this. Cause the Bible does say that the "Soul" never dies; and we know what happens to the body. Then the spirit/soul goes back to GOD. After that, it gets fuzzy for me. But if you read some of the stories especially the ones when kids are talking about, the life they used to have, you'll be convinced that there is definitely something going on.

...and this is why I dedicated this book to my brother.

Keith Brewer (twin)

and pray that GOD release him from the "shackles" of man's crooked system of justice & incarceration…

"…for he without sin, cast the first stone"

My 2nd wife and I were blessed to have 3 daughters. I wanted her to wait to have children (at least 3 or 4 years) but she wasn't having it. She wanted a baby from me, and she wanted it now. So of course I obliged; she was my gorgeous wife. I LOVED her, and there wasn't nothing I wouldn't do for her, or give her. And I think that's how she got involved with the "less of man" she found on face book. She knew I loved her, and loved her unconditionally (so much). And maybe in the deep recess of her "not quite mature" mind she believed I would just let her go with another man and it would be ok. She used to say,

"Well, you forgave your first wife, why can't you forgive me."

And I did forgive the first one; I waited a year. But she never woke up from the mess she ran to. Then the LORD show me in a dream that the marriage was over. I didn't need to wait for her anymore.

And for the 2nd wife; I waited two year; then I prayed and the Lord released me from that one as well. October 2014 was the two year ending of my waiting for her. A few months later I was awaken one morning with her in my thoughts. Then by HIS Spirit, HE released me. When he did, I don't even know where the tears came from. But they caught me off guard. And for about a minute, something left me.

As I was writing these words, the thought came to me that maybe the thing that left me was all the hurt she caused me. And she really did a number. I thought the first wife had a 100 demons towards the end of our marriage, but this wife must have had 10,000. But I will never tell the world all that has been said or done to me by them both. No one would believe it; they would think I was smoking "crack" (which is wack!).

But that is what demonic influence does; it turns your world upside down. It makes you leave your husband, cuss out your mother, turn your back on your Father, care less & abuse your children, sell your body. give it away, degrade yourself, do drugs. love money, hate GOD, and SIN…and that's on a good day.

I guess the truth was (back then) I loved her too much to share. I'm a pretty cool guy, and have always been. I would give my last to anyone, without a problem. Share my time and my space; but two things I never share…my clothes (I'll give it to you first), or pussy (wife). Like I said, I'll give it to you first…So I didn't fight for her.

"I will gladly fight given a reason to do so; but I don't want no one, if they don't feel the same about me, as I about them."

I won't even go into details about that night, or some of the days that followed because it was hard enough living it. So to write about it is just like living it all over again...I DON'T WANT TOO.

After things got pretty bad in the household because she was determine to be with a thug, I was forced to again file for custody of my kids; my 2nd set. Eventually after winning custody of my three girls, my once lovely & beautiful wife resorted to LYING!

She lied; and lied some more; and lied some more; and I wound up in jail. Arrested in a "Chuckie Cheese" in front of my kids; after I agreed to meet her there to see the children.

Did she set me up? Later I found out that she did? As hard as it was to believe, my wife that I would give the world, was now a heartless bitch in love with a wanna-be rapper with an identity problem; not even creative enough to have his own original stage name.

Did I ever doubt that she loved me?

"Nope"

Not even after she sat in the car next to me when she was back and forth between him and I, and told me looking down at the floor,

"I never loved you."

It didn't bother me. My wife has lied all her life; she has even bragged numerous times how good she was at it. Her mother and father taught her well, and she was proud of her little "gift" from them of how to LIE. And living with her as long as we were together at that point (5 years), I knew when she was lying and when she was telling the truth. So her lying to herself was no surprise to me. If this is what she needed to do to justify her actions, then so be it. I knew the real her, and the one I knew was the one I loved, and was proud of. If she didn't love me, I would have never been with her. I had already been married for 13 years with someone I felt didn't love me; & she proved it in the end. I definitely wasn't going to live another LIE with another wife…no matter what.

In spite of all the ugly things she have said to me, said about me, did to me in the end, I knew she loved me. And even if she hates me now; it's only because I refused to share her with some sorry-ass she met on Facebook. To me, she was a beautiful & loving wife that was a great mother to her children. To him, she was just another piece of Ass. And that's what she will always be. He will never trust her (because of her adultery), and she will never trust him. Because she knows he's a "Ho". What they have was not built on Trust. Just Dicks & Pussy (LUST), and LIES, CHEATING, Drugs, and sneaking around. I met her when she was a "proud girl" to bring home to mama. I guess many young people today don't realize that respect only comes with MARRIAGE, not mistress (whore, other woman, Boo).

I have to check my notes of the day I when to jail, but I know I was in there for 11 days while my buddy scrambled around and tried to find a lawyer to bail me out. He eventually found one, but I would have done better with "Mr Magoo" representing me. At least I would still have bank accounts (business & personal), my red mustang I paid cash for, my sailboat, my house, my 4 apartments, my job. Let's just say I met satan's right hand man. I don't know how some of them sleep at night but, it is indeed a shame before GOD what some Lawyers are doing today, and calling it RIGHT.

The Bible says that satan has come to KILL (my spirit), STEAL (everything I worked for), and DESTROY (my life, and the lives of my children)." And he is getting a lot of help from a lot of his unsaved, GOD hating employees.

If I don't have much respect for judges & lawyers (bad ones that is), you can see why. I've had my share of "horrible experiences" of judges & lawyers that have help ruin my life. I'm sure the road to hell will be very crowd with quite a few of them. They have destroyed so many lives, and so many children lives. They have been robbed of their fathers/Daddys; robbed them of their rightful inheritance; just simply destroyed lives. When it comes to that sinister system call C.S. (I won't even spell the word), it makes me sick to the stomach). Just like the heathens that promotes & advocate it (stupid asses)…and I don't even cuss.

WALKING IN THE TARRANT COUNTY JAIL

The detective that took me into custody was a black guy. Of course the way they handled me in "Chuckie Cheese" in front of my 3 daughters and hundreds of other kids was a shame before GOD also. You would have thought I had robbed a bank, killed somebody, are called her a "cunt" and spit in the face of some crooked female judge who hated men. Especially black educated men who know the Law, and know that the law was not bias. Just the people who are supposed to uphold the law, were the bias ones.

Now I've met some nice judges, even know one are two. One I meet years later, and another one I grew up with and is now a judge in my hometown. So all are not bad. Just like all cops, lawyers, and detectives are not all bad. But when you meet one that is, they are "bad to the bone" and need to be "thrown back" like a fish with open sores pulled out of polluted waters. Satan is using them like a "maxi Pad" on a bloody day. And just tosses them to the side after he has used them all up.

When you are arrested, and the charge is sexual, they have a designated area just for sexual offenders. And it doesn't matter if you are as innocent as a 2 year old running around in the back yard naked. You are thrown together with all the harden & career criminals who have made "sex crimes" a career. It's a bit disturbing & embarrassing, but what can you do. The system has arrested you; and there is no such thing as "innocent until proven guilty" even though this is a common belief. And this belief is the biggest joke that our Justice system has played on the criminal, as well as the innocent.

When they put them hand cuffs on you, you are as guilty as Sin according to them; And that is how they ALL treat you.

I had filed for custody of my children, and initially when I won, the wife that I once loved told me,

> *"I'm gonna get you; I'm gonna call the police and say you raped me."*

And that is what she did. I know the idea didn't come from her, because she didn't hate me like that. With her new boyfriend & her mother in her ear, she Lied on the father of her three children. And the husband that she had married after SHE decided to leave Tennessee. Knowing she was rescued from a mother strung-out on crack cocaine, rooming with a fellow crack user that later died from a overdose.

Hurricane Katrina had disrupted many lives, and hers was no exception. When her & her mother along with her brothers were air lifted out, and brought to a shelter in Tennessee, their father refused to leave. So the mother that was once a quiet and submissive wife to a very abusive husband, was now like a wild child sleeping around like she had no husband, and no sense.

And even though there was no hurricane to blame, who would have thought that 6 years later, the daughter would do the same. Also sleep around, like she knew no husband.

But this is the trick of the devil; curses often repeat themselves in the next generation if they do not heed the warnings…and there are always warnings from GOD. If GOD didn't send them, HE wouldn't be GOD.

Looking back on my experiences incarcerated, both occasions were very similar. Each involved a wife that was committing adultery, each wife was now possessed of a demonic spirit, and both lied and painted a horrible picture of me to send me to jail. They both fell for a Trucker that was no good, and made them "no good".

When I was going through this ugly experiences the 2nd time, I remember asking GOD why? Why was I going through this horrible ordeal again? And a voice answered me and said,

"...because you didn't learn the lesson (forgiveness) the first time."

For many years I believed that voice was GOD. But now that I'm older, I wonder if it was GOD? Satan can make things seem real or right, and they be a LIE & WRONG!

At the time, I believed that I had forgiven the first wife. And if I hadn't, surely GOD could just speak to me like HE always does? I could have been spared this last experience...but oh well. I survived.

I was released from jailed after 6 weeks, with no help from the Lawyer that stole my Mustang convertible (U see it on my FB page). The thanks went to GOD & the Grand Jury that obviously looked at all the evidence. Along with the fact that the accuser was my wife, and there was never once a single police call of domestic abuse at our home while together. Since she been with this guy, the police as well as Child Protection have been there many times, and know them both by name.

All charges were dropped against me (no billed), and I was released on the 31st of October 2012. A year to the day that I found out my wife was having an affair with a man her mother gave her the phone number too.

Later after I was released from jailed, she came over to the house with our daughters. She told me,

"You ought to thank me, That man tried to get me to LIE some more to get you convicted & sentenced to 20 years. I told him no, I don't want my children's daddy in no jail for no twenty years."

My response to that response…

"Thank You?; are you tripping? GOD wasn't going to let you & nobody else have me in jail as an innocent man; you must think HE sleeping!"

Some may think it's crazy. But in all the years of preaching, teaching, and learning the Gospel & the things of GOD first hand, straight from the Holy Spirit, I have come to know Demonic possession. And I know both of my wives were possessed toward the end of our relationship. I have forgiven them, and what they don't realize is...it was all satan. Their betrayal & adultery was never about them. It was about me, & the Ministry GOD called me too. And when both wives that I truly loved (the last more than any will ever know) were used by satan to try and destroy me, the plan was for me to quit the Ministry, and not preach the things GOD has told me, and shown me, and taught me. I was Not to think about the many Souls that GOD had appointed unto me. But think only about my SELF. But I refused.

I shook myself off, forgave them both, and continued this journey of being a "Messenger" in these "Last & Evil Days."

In many Churches, I would not be welcomed; but that's not my issue, or problem. Because I know many churches today do not have the Spirit of Almighty GOD. GOD told me recently,

"It is not my job to convince anyone of anything; my job is just to deliver the message that HE placed in my mouth."

When HE said,

"Open up your mouth, & I will give you the words to speak".

So on this note, I bring this message to a closed. It was a story when I started writing it; It is now a Message...I pray that those with ears,."...HEAR.

Many times we don't understand the events in our lives. The day the LORD called me to preached this GOSPEL OF JESUS CHRIST, I looked back and began to understand the events in my Life.

I was called to Preach the Gospel of JESUS CHRIST, and help usher in HIS 2nd Coming. Many Churches today act as if this is a hundred years away, but it's not. The Anti-Christ is on the earth; the current Pope will work with him, and we ARE the Generation that will see JESUS return.

Don't believe me?

It doesn't matter; Just look up, for OUR Redemption draws nigh…

…I AM, SIR…the SOULman

"Making Reservations for Souls to return to GOD (in Heaven)"

If you want a reservation, I can help you make arrangements. If you don't, that's OK too…I'll just PRAY…like I always do. And GOD will HEAR ME…and ANSWER. HE promised me, …that HE would.

(Finis)

French for THE END

26.   And the spirit cried; rent him sore, and came out of him: and he was as one dead; In so much that many said, He is dead.

27.   But JESUS took him by the hand, and lifted him up; and he arose.

28.   And when he was come into the house, his disciples asked him privately, Why could we not cast him out?

29. And he said unto them, *This kind can come forth by nothing but by prayer and fasting*

MARK Chapter 9

Just Another Messenger of GOD

www.ingramcontent.com/pod-product-compliance
Lightning Source LLC
Chambersburg PA
CBHW061507040426
42450CB00008B/1514